CAREER AS A

CRIMINAL DEFENSE LAWYER

IN THE UNITED STATES CRIMINAL JUSTICE SYSTEM, those charged with a crime are entitled to a defense. The people responsible for providing that defense, as well as protecting the rights of the accused, are skilled attorneys, known as criminal defense lawyers.

Mounting a case for a criminal defendant can be an awesome task, fraught with numerous pitfalls and obstacles. In an effort to prove that a client is innocent, a defense attorney has to battle the full power of the state or federal government, which is often backed by a determined force of law enforcement agents.

The role of criminal defense attorneys is extremely important in the criminal justice system because defense lawyers keep the system honest, making sure there truly is justice for all. When lawyers take on a case on behalf of the defense, it is their job to make sure that evidence was gathered properly and legally, confessions were not coerced, searches were conducted to the letter of the law, testimony was not fabricated, and the rights of the suspect were not violated in any way.

The defense attorney may be the only one in an overburdened criminal justice system advocating for the accused. Defense attorneys see the accused not as a docket number, but rather as a person with rights and a voice to be heard. Wealthy or indigent, all clients must be treated equally by defense attorneys, who make sure that those bringing charges against any client meet the burden of proof.

A great deal is at stake here. A wrongful conviction can ruin a client's life. There is little room for error.

Defense attorneys handle cases from misdemeanors to felonies. A convicted client can receive a punishment ranging from a fine, to community service, probation, several years in prison, or even life imprisonment. In some cases, the death penalty is on the table.

No matter what the severity of the crime, defense attorneys represent people in what is often their darkest hour. Criminal law is complex, with each state enacting its own criminal laws and setting its own punishments. Some crimes are covered by federal laws as well.

Most criminal cases do not make sensational headlines in the daily newspapers or get spotlighted on network and cable news or online news sites. These cases are just as important to the people charged with that crime as the cases that captivate the public's attention. Regardless of the notoriety the case gets, little attention is paid to the hard work and long hours defense attorneys put in behind the scenes, working every angle to get their clients off or to minimize their sentences.

Most people are only aware of the time defense counsel spends arguing a case in court. There will also be months or even years of work that go into a case, and that case is hardly ever the only one the attorney is working on.

When you choose to become a criminal defense attorney, you are embarking on a fascinating and demanding career. In this profession, you will be seeking out the truth and representing your client to the best of your ability, while seeing to it that justice is served.

WHAT YOU CAN DO NOW

THERE ARE PLENTY OF OPPORTUNITIES to watch criminal defense attorneys in action by going down to a courtroom near you, whether it is a municipal, county, state, or federal court. This will give you the chance to see how arguments are made, evidence is presented, and witnesses are questioned, as well as observing the jury, the defendant, and the judge.

A criminal trial is a pressure-filled atmosphere. You will feel the intensity when you are in the courtroom. Sitting in on a trial will give you a chance to see if you think you would be comfortable working in this kind of adversarial setting.

To get an in-depth look at what it is like to represent someone accused of a crime, try to make an appointment with a defense attorney to talk about the job and all the aspects of mounting a defense in a criminal trial. Many public defenders would be willing to give you a glimpse of their tireless efforts to represent those accused of a crime but who are unable to afford an attorney. You might be able to volunteer in the public defender's office to gain even greater insight into this work.

Well-known defense attorneys have written informative books, and reading those will give you an insider's perspective on criminal defense law. *The Defense Never Rests,* by F. Lee Bailey, reviews some of that noted defense attorney's most controversial cases, including the Boston Strangler case. Defense attorney Abbe Smith's book, *Case of a Lifetime: A Criminal Defense Lawyer's Story*, is another good study about defending both the guilty and the innocent. Journalist Kevin Davis gives everyone a reality check in his book about public defenders in Chicago, in *Defending the Damned: Inside a Dark Corner of the Criminal Justice System*.

HISTORY OF THE CAREER

"THE TRIAL OF THE CENTURY" THAT IS A PHASE used by the news media to describe a courtroom drama that captivates the public. It usually refers to criminal cases.

Sensational, headline-grabbing trials, like those of O. J. Simpson (1995), Sam Sheppard (1950s-1960s), the Lindbergh baby kidnapper (1935), the Scottsboro Boys (1930s), and John Hinckley Jr. (1982), have all been called "trial of the century." As the list implies, more than a few cases have earned this title. These legal proceedings involve defendants, usually viewed by the public with contempt and disdain, and well-known lawyers, especially criminal defense attorneys. Which case actually qualifies as *the* trial of the past one hundred years is up for debate, but it shows the high regard in which criminal cases are held in history and our society.

Criminal law dates back thousands of years. The earliest known code of criminal laws is believed to have been written between 2100 and 2050 BC by the Sumerians, who lived in present-day Iraq.

In the United States, the roots of the legal system, including criminal law, can be traced back to England. Criminal law has evolved quite a bit in the United States since colonial times, but long before the American Revolution, criminal defense attorneys represented clients accused of crimes in what became the United

States. Some of those lawyers got their legal training in England.

Among the most famous pre-Revolutionary War criminal trials held in the colonies were the cases against British captain Thomas Preston and eight men under his command. The captain and his men were accused of shooting and killing five Boston residents during a raucous gathering outside the Custom House in Boston on March 5, 1770. The event became known as the Boston Massacre. If they had been convicted, Preston and those eight troops under his command could have faced the death penalty.

Lawyer after lawyer in the colonies refused to represent the British troops. Finally, Massachusetts attorney John Adams, a fierce American patriot, took the case. He did so based on his belief that everyone deserves a fair trial. His defense of Preston was built around the argument that the officer never gave an order to fire into the crowd. While the prosecution presented witnesses who testified that Preston did give the order to shoot, Adams had close to two dozen convincing witnesses who claimed the captain never gave such an order. Preston was acquitted based on reasonable doubt.

The charges against the eight soldiers were addressed in a separate trial. Adams based his defense in that case on the soldiers having been provoked by the crowd's rowdy behavior and claimed the military men feared for their lives. Six of the soldiers were acquitted and two were found guilty of manslaughter, rather than murder. The manslaughter convictions allowed for leniency and the two soldiers were able to avoid long prison terms.

As a result of the trials, Adams became known as one of the nation's best criminal defense attorneys and legal minds. The Boston Massacre trials proved the value of a good criminal defense attorney to the accused, and the importance of a fair trial.

Once the 13 colonies won their independence from England in 1783, the framers of the US Constitution felt that one of the paramount concerns of the new nation was protecting the rights of individuals accused of a crime. As a result, the US Constitution (adopted in 1789) and the Bill of Rights (ratified in 1791) contain a series of measures to address that issue, including the right to a fair trial, to a jury trial, to due process, to be informed of all charges and evidence, and to have an attorney, as well as protection from unreasonable searches and seizures, double jeopardy, self-incrimination, excessive bail, and cruel and unusual punishment.

Through the centuries that followed, it fell to the nation's court system, most notably the US Supreme Court to make sure these provisions were being interpreted properly and that the rights of the accused were being upheld. Many important Supreme Court decisions have impacted criminal law and have given criminal defense lawyers the tools they need. The rights of the accused came into extremely sharp focus between 1961 and 1969. In that period, several key decisions involving the rights of the accused were handed down by the High Court.

- Mapp v. Ohio (1961), makes all evidence gathered through an unreasonable search and seizure in violation of the Fourth Amendment to the Constitution inadmissible in state court cases.

- Brady v. Maryland (1963), requires the prosecution to disclose to the defense material exculpatory evidence.

- Gideon v. Wainwright (1963), makes it mandatory for states to provide a lawyer to a criminal defendant who is unable to afford an attorney.

- Miranda v. Arizona (1966), ensures that suspects be informed of their rights, including the right to remain silent and to an attorney before and during questioning.

These history-making decisions, which helped shape criminal procedure in the United States, came about due to the dogged determination of dedicated criminal defense attorneys.

WHERE YOU WILL WORK

CRIMINAL DEFENSE ATTORNEYS ARE NEEDED everywhere in the country, from sparsely populated rural areas to big cities with growing populations.

Wherever you decide to set up your criminal law practice, you will be splitting your time between the office and the courtroom. Most criminal defense attorneys look for office space close to the courthouse where the majority of their cases will be heard and where they meet with prosecutors. You will be going to other places as well, including crime scenes, and perhaps even visiting your clients in jail. This is not legal work for the squeamish.

Many high-profile cases are taken up by large law firms, located in big cities. These law firms often employ hundreds of lawyers, as well as support staff. They have impressive names on their letterhead, stylish offices, and a hefty price tag for their services.

These are good places to learn the ropes and build a reputation, but at one of these prestigious law firms, it may take you a while to become lead attorney in a major criminal case. You will work with a team of attorneys on most of the cases you are assigned. You will be called on to research some of the finer points of the law in the law library, while your associates are doing the same thing on other aspects of the case.

Large law firms offer the advantage of having vast resources at their disposal, and clients who can afford to pay for those extras that help chip away at a prosecutor's case. These law firms also get a wide range of cases, from murders that have been well publicized to minor drug offenses, so you have an opportunity to see how all these cases are handled. These upper-echelon law firms can be found anywhere in the country, but they are most often located in major cities, like New York, Chicago, Los Angeles, and Atlanta, where people are willing to pay top dollar for the best services.

If the mega-law firm scene does not appeal to you, there are plenty of small and midsized law firms all over the nation that handle a variety of criminal law cases. These law firms have smaller staffs, and that means more work for each attorney. You may start handling bigger cases sooner and you will have a better chance of developing a good track record that can lead to a partnership.

Even though it can be difficult for a young lawyer just starting out, you may want to become a sole practitioner, opening your own office. Many sole practitioners take on cases nobody else wants and clients with limited means. You will end up working just as hard to build up your clientele and provide good legal services as you would if you were an associate in an established law firm.

You could also work in the public defender's office. Public defenders are criminal defense attorneys paid with public funds to represent indigent clients.

THE WORK YOU WILL DO

THE VERDICT IS IN: YOU HAVE SET YOUR SIGHTS on becoming a criminal defense attorney. There is much more to this job than giving thought-provoking opening statements, conducting riveting cross-examinations, and making stirring closing arguments. What you do behind the scenes can often make – or break – your whole case.

The work may start even before an arrest is made. A person suspected of a crime might hire a criminal defense attorney when police are just beginning their investigation. At this stage, you need to keep your client from making any self-incriminating statements to investigators. While police are investigating the crime, you are consulting with your client to learn everything you can about his/her side of the story. You can then advise your client about how to respond when answering questions from the authorities.

The most important part of your job now is to make sure that police follow procedure and your client's rights are not violated in any way. On rare occasions, after the police have conducted their investigation and have come up with little evidence incriminating your client, you can persuade the authorities to drop the case and not press any charges.

If your client is arrested, you will probably be summoned to the police station to be present while police are questioning your client. Within a reasonable time following an arrest, your client will be arraigned. You will appear in court with your client for the arraignment. At this point your client will be formally told what he/she is being charged with, and will be asked to enter a plea. In most jurisdictions, if your client pleads not guilty at the arraignment, the court will decide if he/she will be released on bail. This is when you present arguments to get your client out on the lowest possible bail or, if possible, on recognizance.

Now you begin to develop your case for a court hearing. At this juncture, criminal defense attorneys start gathering and analyzing all the information associated with the case. That includes reviewing police reports and witness statements, and examining any evidence collected in connection with the crime. Once you have gone over everything thoroughly, you must identify the strengths and weaknesses of the case to try to poke holes in the case against your client. You will talk with your client many times throughout this period, reviewing the evidence and getting your client's explanation for what the authorities found that links him/her to the crime.

Most experienced criminal defense attorneys will visit the crime scene as part of the preparation for going to court. This helps put the case in context, gives you familiarity with the crime scene, and gives you the background you need to conduct an in-depth cross-examination of some of the witnesses the prosecution will put on the witness stand. A visit to the crime scene may also enable you to see something that might bolster your client's case. A witness for the prosecution might claim that she saw something while standing in a particular place when the crime was committed. But when you go to the scene, you realize that the witness simply could not have had a clear view of what was going on if she was standing where she claimed to be. Now you can challenge the witness's story and begin to create some reasonable doubt. Remember: You do not have to prove that your client is innocent, but simply that there is a "reasonable doubt" as to whether he/she committed the crime.

If you come across witnesses who support your client's version of the story, you have to talk to them and decide if you want to put them on the witness stand to testify during the trial. For example, your client may have an alibi and you need to check out that story and see if anyone can corroborate it. If someone can, then you have to determine if that person would be a credible witness on behalf of your client.

Preparing witnesses to testify in court is no easy task. Naturally, you know the questions you are going to ask and can prepare witnesses to answer those questions. But you do not know the questions the prosecuting attorney will ask. As part of witness preparation, you have to imagine how you would question the witness on the stand if you were the prosecuting attorney. You do not want your witnesses – the witnesses for the defense – to falter while testifying and say anything you do not anticipate. Criminal defense attorneys seek to prepare their witnesses for anything, knowing that the prosecutor will try to break a defense witness's story and attack the witness's credibility. The best way to avoid having witnesses look bad on the stand is to make sure they know what to expect and are ready for whatever the prosecution throws their way. Witness preparation can take days, until a witness gains the confidence needed to handle questioning under rigorous cross-examination.

At the trial, you will be arguing against a prosecutor. In some jurisdictions, prosecutors are called district attorneys. Though you are both dealing with the same incident, you will be telling the story from different perspectives. The prosecutor will be trying to prove that your client committed the crime. You will be presenting a different scenario, one where your client did not commit the crime.

As a criminal defense attorney, you will be involved in selecting people for a jury in the case you are handling. You want people on the jury who will be impartial or might even lean toward your client, as opposed to individuals who seem as though they believe that anyone who is charged with a crime is guilty and will dismiss your arguments out of hand.

During trial preparation or while the trial is going on, you may come across evidence the prosecution has that you feel should not be presented at trial. Criminal defense attorneys spend a great deal of time writing motions, supported by case law, in an attempt to suppress certain evidence that might compromise their client's case. Writing these motions requires intensive research to find legal precedents to convince a judge to side with the defense. Criminal defense attorneys write other motions as well, including motions to dismiss a charge or to dismiss the entire case if the attorney feels there is insufficient evidence to support the charges or make the case. The judge then rules on each motion.

You will also write and rewrite and rewrite your opening statements and closing arguments. This is much more than just a writing assignment. You will bring these words to life in court as you use gripping oratory to spell out your case in front of the jury in your opening statement. Then at the end of the trial, you will review your case in spellbinding form in your closing argument as you make your final push to convince the jury of your client's innocence. Your job is to captivate the jury, have them hang on your every word, and arrive at a "not guilty" verdict.

One of the biggest decisions you will have to make is whether to have your client testify. Various factors figure in this decision, including whether your client has a criminal or shady past and will be believable. Many times members of a jury will wonder why a defendant did not testify, and a prosecutor may exploit that fact. Sometimes, having your client testify during a trial can actually undermine your case. Your client might not be likable, might come across as having a bad attitude, or might show disdain for the criminal justice system. Criminal defense attorneys sometimes wrestle with the question of whether to put a client on the witness stand right up to the last possible moment they have to make the decision.

As a trial is proceeding, and the prosecution is making its case and calling its witnesses, the criminal defense attorney is taking copious notes. Before a particular prosecution witness is called, you might think that you want to attack that person's testimony one way. But after you hear what the witness says on the stand, you might come up with a different strategy. You have to be able to make that adjustment flawlessly and often on the fly. Your notes will become critical to your cross-examination as you pick out salient points in the prosecution witness's testimony that you want to attack.

Every evening following a day in court, criminal defense attorneys carefully study their notes from the day's courtroom activity as they get ready for the next day's testimony. These attorneys work long hours following the day's proceedings.

If your client is found guilty, you will play a major role at the sentencing, trying to convince the judge to be lenient and explaining the reasons why. You may even offer an alternative to incarceration that may give your client an opportunity for rehabilitation and a chance to become a productive member of society.

Following a guilty verdict, your client might want to appeal the case to a higher court. An appeal is a review of the lower court's actions in an attempt to get the conviction overturned or a sentence reduced. In making an appeal, which is a lengthy process, a criminal defense attorney spends more time reviewing transcripts of the trial and case law than actual time in court. Sound arguments have to be put together in an appellate brief to convince the appeals court that errors were made during the lower-court trial and a remedy is in order. Keep in mind that the prosecutor often files a rebuttal to the defense attorney's appellate brief.

Many times, criminal cases do not go to trial. While you are preparing your case to go to court, the prosecutor may contact you and make a plea offer. As a criminal defense attorney, you must discuss any plea offers with your client. You can make a recommendation, but it is ultimately up to your client to decide whether to accept the plea deal or take a chance in court. At times, your client will admit guilt and the evidence is overwhelming. This is where your negotiating skills will come into play. It is helpful to speak to your client at this point and see if any mitigating circumstances led up to the crime, such as alcohol addiction, that might make the person a candidate for a rehabilitation program, rather than a jail term. If property was damaged or merchandise stolen, you might be able to work out a restitution program and keep your client from spending any time in prison.

Even though the court calendar is filled with cases, that does not mean the prosecutor is going to accept any plea offer you make, just to clear the calendar. In fact, prosecutors often do not accept your first offer. Plea negotiation involves a great deal of give-and-take, and you have to make a convincing case for leniency when you try to work out a plea bargain. You may not get the deal you want. Then you have to return to your client and discuss the pros and cons of the plea bargain being offered. You can still make a counteroffer, or your client could decide to take a chance at trial. The toughest part of this job is that you are in a profession where people's lives and futures are on the line every day, and the outcome depends in large measure on your efforts.

LAWYERS TELL THEIR OWN STORIES

I Am a Criminal Defense Attorney in a Rural Area

"When I got out of law school roughly 20 years ago, jobs for lawyers were hard to come by and I kept hearing people in the legal field say, 'Go rural – they need lawyers there.' So I decided to give it a try.

I always had an interest in being a criminal defense attorney and I found, even a bit to my surprise, that I was able to provide my services to many of the people who lived in the rural community I finally decided to settle in. I never got a lot of cases for what people would consider serious crimes, like murder, but there are still plenty of people in need of quality representation for drug offenses, driving under the influence (DUI), domestic violence, minor assaults, and thefts. Many folks around here would need help if one of their kids got into some trouble or they themselves got into a tussle with the law.

When you live here a while, people get to know you and they trust you and that's a big plus. I've also had many cases involving people who were passing through the area, a crime was committed, they got charged with it, and suddenly they needed a criminal defense attorney.

I like the time element involved in working in a rural area. Things move a bit more slowly out here, and that gives me more time to spend with each client and to explore every angle of a case.

I'm a big believer in second chances, especially when it comes to kids, and I can do that here. I can work out a lighter sentence, maybe get a charge expunged after a while, and watch a life turn around.

I don't represent many hardened criminals and I don't mind that. However, with drugs and DUI you do get many repeat offenders. I've had some pretty serious crimes on occasion and I was ready and able to handle that kind of case.

In rural areas, you find there can easily be a miscarriage of justice in a major criminal case, especially if the accused is from out of the area. Police and prosecutors can get overzealous in their attempt to solve a crime, charge someone, and get a conviction. They don't constantly handle major criminal cases, so they can get sloppy, inadvertently violate someone's rights, try to make the pieces of the puzzle fit together when they really don't. I'm here to make sure that doesn't happen. While I'm part of the community and want to keep it safe, I am not here to rubber-stamp whatever law enforcement and the prosecutor does. In fact, I am constantly challenging it.

I can say that as a criminal defense attorney I've seen it all in my career in rural America, though to a limited extent. There's lots of work in these areas. People are grateful you are here, and while you might not earn as much money as criminal defense attorneys in a big city, the cost of living is cheaper, especially when it comes to expenses like renting office space."

I Am a Criminal Defense Attorney in a Large Law Firm

"OK, you can get ready to dislike me. I represent people accused of murder, sexual assault, vicious aggravated assaults, and armed robberies, among other terrible crimes. When most folks hear what my clients are accused of doing, they say. 'How can you defend those people?'

First of all, not everyone who is arrested is guilty as charged. Maybe the person didn't do it. Part of my job is making sure prosecutors meet their burden of proof and have charged the right person.

Even if my client did commit a crime, I'm not defending the crime – I'm defending my client's rights. That's very important. If there is no one there to stand up for the accused, the state can easily trample on people's rights and wrongfully rack up one conviction after another with evidence that wasn't collected properly or witnesses who lied to get some kind of deal for themselves.

I provide the checks and balances in the system. Every year thousands of people are wrongfully convicted of crimes they didn't commit and I am out to stop at least some of that. Criminal law is complicated and there are many laws that were put on the books with good reason to protect the rights of the accused. I make sure those laws are followed to the letter. We are dealing with people's lives here and criminal defense attorneys have to make sure the police and prosecutors don't take any shortcuts, make mistakes, mishandle evidence, or are just lazy when handling a case.

As a criminal defense attorney, you make sure people don't just plead guilty to something simply to get it over with. Sometimes these people think, 'Well, the system is out to get me anyway. What difference does it make?' But there are consequences to taking a guilty plea so you can move on with your life, especially if you aren't guilty but don't see any other way out of the mess except to accept a guilty plea and cut your losses. If you plead guilty, you get a criminal record. That record will be taken into consideration if you are ever accused of another crime later on in life, or apply for a job or a loan. It reflects badly on your family.

Maybe you are guilty but there are mitigating circumstances the court should know about, like a drug addiction or a psychological problem. Perhaps you should be put in a program and get cured, rather than a jail cell. A good defense attorney can get the court to understand those mitigating circumstances and persuade the court to go along with an alternative to incarceration.

Too often we see articles in the newspaper about people released after spending years in prison when modern DNA testing proved them innocent. That means the police arrested the wrong person. The district attorney prosecuted the wrong person, and the wrong person lost years of life in prison. We can't get those years back. That can't be fixed.

Our job is to do everything possible to make sure that never happens, to rigorously put the system to the test every day. To make law enforcement and prosecutors prove to you and the court that they've got the right person. To dig into their investigation, challenge their case, and leave no stone unturned to be sure justice is being served for everyone involved in the case."

I Am a Public Defender

"Working as a public defender is the best way to learn how to be a good criminal defense lawyer. This is a challenging job and you are thrown into the fray right away.

The public defender's office has few resources, so you are working at a great disadvantage. Think about it: Prosecutors have a staff, their own investigators, police departments at their disposal, and everybody views them as the good guys. The public defender's office has none of that, so you have to be committed to the work. Your priority has to be to protect the rights of the accused. I've had people who have been wrongly accused, mistakenly identified by a confused witness, and I've gotten those people off. That makes the job worthwhile.

I've also had people who are constant repeat offenders – they just don't care about right and wrong or what happens to their victims. That's frustrating. Even though you know these people committed the crimes they were charged with, you still have to make sure their rights are not violated in any way and you need to present the best defense possible.

Then there are those people who made one bad decision. You know they've learned their lesson and you work hard to get them a sentence that might give them a chance to get their lives back together. If you do, that gives you a good feeling, especially if you see a person down the road, who took advantage of that second chance and is doing well.

You are going to be representing many guilty people. A public defender doesn't get a chance to choose clients, so you have to learn how to work with all kinds of personalities and attitudes. Some respect you and what you are trying to do for them, but others don't. I work equally hard for all my clients, but some look at you as a hired hand for a system that just wants to put them in jail.

Having thick skin is a big part of the job. You can't let the criticism bother you. Police officers will get angry at you for a variety of reasons – like the way you question them on the stand or because you defend people they've arrested and believe are guilty. You've got to be able to let that roll off. You're doing your job, just like the police.

Being a public defender can be stressful. I want to see the innocent get off. There is a lot of work. The cases never stop coming in, but you do get hours and hours of trial and courtroom experience. There's nothing you don't see and you gain tons of confidence. I don't have any jitters when I go into the courtroom now and when I think I have a case I can win, I go for it. When I believe I have a valid point, I pursue it. Public defenders learn to be fearless advocates, and that is something that can help you in all aspects of life."

PERSONAL QUALIFICATIONS

JUST HOW PERSUASIVE ARE YOU? CAN you make an argument, back it up with facts, and get people with either a different point of view or no opinion at all to side with you? That is a trait you must have in order to be a good criminal defense attorney.

During your career as a criminal defense attorney, your job will often come down to how well you can make your argument. Getting your point across convincingly means striking a delicate balance when presenting your case. You have to be authoritative yet not overbearing, confident but not arrogant, firm in your beliefs but not preachy.

Many cases are won by a strong closing argument that dissects and exposes the flaws in the prosecution's case, offering a jury or a judge a viable alternative to the charges being made against your client. Do not forget: You only have to create a reasonable doubt.

Criminal defense attorneys must be good public speakers. They have to engage a jury and a judge, and be sincere and likable when speaking in court.

Often overlooked as an important tool in a criminal defense attorney's arsenal are listening skills. By noting everything that goes on in court, you figure out ways to challenge the opposition's case. You also have to listen to what your clients tell you, as well as witnesses, investigating police officers, anyone involved in the case. Are you convinced by what they say? Do you pick up on the full import of their account? Are they holding anything back? Listening attentively allows you to read between the lines and seize on salient points others might miss.

Being well organized is crucial. You have to be able to put your finger on key material immediately, and avoid having to scout around looking for something you scribbled on a scrap of paper and then cannot find.

If you like to think fast, this is the job for you. Hearing something in court, reacting to it, then changing your approach; asking the right questions, even if a witness testifying in court says something that takes you by surprise – these are invaluable qualities for any criminal defense attorney.

In this job you cannot get flustered or be left flat-footed. It is hard to recover from something like that. You avoid that by doing extensive preparation when representing your client, whether it is in court or in a plea negotiation. That requires analytical thinking. As a criminal defense attorney, you have to think about the case from all angles. You eat, drink, and sleep these cases and try to anticipate anything the prosecution can hit you with.

Being a good negotiator will help your clients over and over again. Sometimes, after you have completely reviewed a case, you realize that there is just no way you can get your client off without some kind of punishment. Minimizing the sentence is now the option you must pursue and your negotiating skills will determine whether your client receives a long or a reduced sentence.

ATTRACTIVE FEATURES

CRUSADING FOR JUSTICE IS A ROLE many criminal defense attorneys relish. Representing the downtrodden – serving as a voice for the voiceless – is a noble cause, even if your client is guilty. It makes you a defender of the US Constitution, which guarantees in the Sixth Amendment everyone's right to legal counsel when charged with a crime. So, in essence, you are putting into practice the principles set forth by the nation's founders.

Being a criminal defense attorney is an exciting career, filled with drama both inside and outside the courtroom. Boredom seldom sets in. You are always on the move in this action-packed career.

Though many crimes are similar, rarely are two exactly alike. Each criminal case involves a different twist and that keeps you on your toes. Criminal defense law is one of the more creative branches of the legal field because you can always find new and cutting-edge ways to defend your client. You might discover mitigating circumstances that were not present in another case, a defense that is more plausible in one case than another, an alibi for your client that was never looked into by the police, or an entirely different scenario of the crime, with witnesses to back it up, that the police failed to pursue. These kinds of challenges make the job so worthwhile and satisfying when you put on a winning defense.

This field of law gives you an opportunity to distinguish yourself as both a litigator and an orator. You have the power to sway a jury, to get people to look at a case from your perspective.

If working in a competitive atmosphere gets you excited, this is the job for you. You can put your skills on display against the best prosecutors, find the weaknesses in a prosecutor's case, capitalize on a key mistake made by your opponent, and win the day.

As a defense attorney, you can stand up against authority every day. You are the one making sure your client does not fall prey to police officers or prosecutors who rush to judgment.

Good criminal defense attorneys never stop learning, and the advent of new types of criminal activity, such as cyber-crime, requires you to come up with new ways of defending people charged with these crimes.

Daring attorneys who develop well-thought-out criminal defenses have a chance to gain a great deal of fame and fortune. Even those who represent the underprivileged and may not receive a large fee can be recognized for their work if it is groundbreaking. That can lead to other ways of making money, like writing books, teaching criminal defense law at a leading law school, or going on the lecture circuit talking about some of your most notable cases.

Extremely gifted and determined criminal defense attorneys can put their expertise to work to help wrongly convicted people get out of jail by working with organizations like the Innocence Project. What could be more rewarding than that?

UNATTRACTIVE ASPECTS

AS A CRIMINAL DEFENSE ATTORNEY, you see the seedy side of life almost every day. The world can be a mean place, and while you may not be right on the front lines, you are pretty close.

Many of the cases you handle are heartbreaking, from the standpoint of both the accused and the victim. You hear about people's inhumanity against each other all the time and after a while it can be difficult to keep from getting bitter.

As a lawyer, you win some cases and you lose some cases, but most criminal defense lawyers lose many more than they win. It does not hurt as much when you know your client is guilty, but when your client is innocent, that can be very upsetting.

Studies claim that thousands of people are wrongfully convicted of crimes in the United States every year. One study reports the number of wrongful convictions as high as 10,000 annually. Many factors underlie these wrongful convictions, including witnesses who could exonerate a defendant failing to come forward, and the inability to locate a key piece of evidence that would prove a person's innocence. Recognizing that your client may be wrongly convicted, despite your best efforts, is a very frustrating part of a career as a criminal defense lawyer.

Representing a client you know is guilty may be distasteful and sometimes cause you a crisis of conscience. If the prosecution has a weak case or a guilty client's rights have been violated, it is your duty to go after the state's case vigorously and get your client off. It can be extremely troubling knowing you put a guilty person back on the streets, but that is what you need to do in the interests of justice when the rights of the accused have been trampled on or there just is not enough evidence to convict your client.

Criminal defense attorneys spend a great deal of time in court, which is an extremely stressful environment. In an attempt to give your client a strong defense, you often have to aggressively question police officers and tear into crime victims on the stand. No matter how much you may empathize with these individuals, you still must forcefully go after them. That certainly makes you look like a cold and callous individual, an image you might not be comfortable with.

Some of your clients might be unrepentant and unremorseful and have committed heinous criminal acts. The egregiousness of those acts makes the public hate you for defending them as much as they hate the criminals.

Some prosecutors can be very hard-nosed. They are only interested in the convictions they amass and the tough sentences they get judges to impose. Being known as a hard-hitting law enforcer is all that matters to them. These kinds of prosecutors are difficult to deal with, especially when it comes to forging a plea bargain. They often insist on long sentences for people who commit minor offenses, when justice would be better served by giving those people probation or community service.

EDUCATION AND TRAINING

YOU WILL FIND MANY GOOD LAW SCHOOLS throughout the country. US News & World Report ranks them every year, and so does Law Street, the web-based media site that covers the world of law. Boston College Law School has a very good website that can give you some valuable insights when deciding which law schools to apply to.

What sets these law schools apart is how each school addresses the legal specialty you want to go into. So the best law school for someone who wants to become a criminal defense attorney is one that offers research opportunities in criminal law as well as internships with criminal law judges and criminal defense lawyers.

Even more important is making sure that the law school has a good legal clinic that focuses on criminal cases. Law school legal clinics provide pro bono (no fee) work for low-income clients and give law students a chance to get hands-on experience in a variety of legal specialties. Criminal law is one of the prime specialties for law school legal clinics, since so many people accused of crimes need legal representation but cannot afford it. Today, it is about more than just getting into law school. It is about getting into a law school that has a good, solid program that combines traditional classroom learning with real-world, on-the-job professional experience.

Take the time to study the legal clinics these schools offer to the public. The clinics are the hidden jewels at these law schools. At these clinics, you can roll up your sleeves, get into the middle of the action, test yourself, gain courtroom experience, help people, and have a chance to meet an experienced criminal defense attorney who might be interested in mentoring you. Many top criminal defense attorneys volunteer at these clinics and help law students with the cases that come in. Good mentors are hard to find, but they are the best way to learn the business and get a foot in the door in this exciting aspect of the law.

Keep in mind that the way law is taught at these schools varies, and the way their law clinics operate varies as well. For example, at the criminal defense clinic at the University of Virginia School of Law in Charlottesville, law students learn the strategies, techniques, and responsibilities of representing clients. Students handle actual criminal cases in local courts. The law students are supervised by experienced criminal defense attorneys who help guide them through the process and offer practical advice, although the students do all the work, including interviewing clients and witnesses, reviewing evidence, preparing the case, making motions, negotiating pleas, and handling all other aspects of the case.

The University of Connecticut School of Law in Hartford has two criminal law clinics – a trial clinic and an appellate clinic. The clinics are run by supervising professors, but the goal is for students to undertake all the work on behalf of the indigent clients who turn to the clinics for help. The aim of each clinic is to provide the highest caliber of criminal defense work while meeting the needs of each client.

More than 20 law clinics comprise the Bluhm Legal Clinic at Northwestern University Pritzker School of Law in Chicago. The

Center for Criminal Defense, one of those clinics, allows students to fine-tune their skills by representing adult clients charged with crimes in venues throughout Illinois. The students handle cases in federal courts as well. The work involves motions, jury trials, and advocacy at sentencing. Among the other clinics at the school are the Center on Wrongful Convictions, the Children and Family Justice Center, and the Appellate Advocacy Center.

These are just a few of the law schools with law clinics that give students an edge in gaining practical skills while still in school. Their peers, who have not had training at a law school legal clinic, might need years to hone these same skills as professionals. Typically second- and third-year law students can participate in these clinics, but it varies from law school to law school.

Going to law school requires first earning an undergraduate college degree. People come to law school and the field of law with all types of undergraduate degrees. So you might want to take something you like as an undergraduate that would prepare you for another career if law school does not work out.

Getting into law school depends on your grade point average and your scores on the Law School Admission Test (LSAT). Prospective law school students usually take the LSAT in their junior year in college. You can take the test more than once to improve your scores and your chances of getting into the law school you want.

Keep in mind that if you go to law school full time, it takes three years to get your degree.

EARNINGS

MANY FACTORS HAVE TO BE TAKEN INTO ACCOUNT when determining what a private criminal defense attorney earns on an annual basis. It usually comes down to how many cases the attorney takes on in a year, the billable hours involved with those cases, and the financial bracket of the clients being represented.

The average yearly earnings nationwide of a criminal defense attorney working as an associate in a private law practice are roughly $150,000, with associates considered top-notch and in high demand commanding annual salaries of upwards of $300,000. That is for lawyers with five years of experience. The national average for partners in these law firms reaches $600,000-plus, but that varies with the size of the firm.

Young criminal defense attorneys just starting out at big law firms usually bring home annual paychecks in the $65,000 to $75,000 range, with small law firms starting their associates out at about $50,000 yearly. There are geographic differentials as well, with criminal defense attorneys in major cities like New York City, Chicago, Los Angeles, and Dallas earning 10 to 15 percent more than their counterparts in smaller, less-populated areas.

Salaries for public defenders vary greatly, depending on the budget for the public defender's office where they work. Those budgets are determined by taxpayer dollars and that funding is shrinking in many jurisdictions. The pay scale for public defenders is about $40,000 to $50,000 a year. The chief public defender, usually a very experienced criminal defense attorney, can make as much as $90,000.

OPPORTUNITIES

CRIMINAL DEFENSE ATTORNEYS WILL ALWAYS be in demand. No matter whether crime is up or down, all people accused of a crime need representation. Hardly anyone but a criminal defense attorney is well versed enough in the law to go into court and mount a competent defense against a criminal charge. In other words, a layman cannot do it. Representing yourself is a guaranteed losing proposition, so calling a professional is the only sensible option.

Criminal defense law is a highly competitive field, but there is no shortage of those who need your services. The court dockets are full, and many people are in jail waiting for their day in court. In addition, a number of people convicted of a crime want their cases appealed. This all speaks well about how much work is out there to keep attorneys very busy.

Criminal defense is a branch of the law profession that requires dogged determination, both to succeed as a career and to win cases. If you have the tenacity to stick with it, you have a good chance of carving out a nice niche for yourself in this field. Some criminal attorneys build a lucrative practice by representing people accused of particular types of crimes, like drug-related offenses or white-collar crimes. Like any other business, it is important to study the profession in your area and see where the need is greatest for criminal defense attorneys, and where you can make your mark.

Interestingly, every year the FBI releases a report listing the areas of the country with the most crime. Many lawyers thinking about going into a criminal defense law practice use that information to figure out which regions are in the greatest need of criminal defense lawyers.

An interesting study was recently released by Western New England University School of Law that is very positive for the job outlook picture for young attorneys. The report concludes that a robust job market for lawyers is on the horizon. According to the report, an additional 166,000 lawyers will be needed in the United States, based on current population growth.

Lawyers retiring from the profession will create additional job opportunities for young lawyers. More than a half a million lawyers now employed will retire by the year 2030, and the retirement rate may even go higher than that. Criminal defense attorneys will be among the positions that will need to be filled.

GETTING STARTED

MANY YOUNG ATTORNEYS WHO WANT to go into criminal defense work begin their careers by working for the opposition. Putting in several years as a prosecuting attorney, working in a district attorney's office, may seem like a strange way to cut your teeth in criminal defense, but it gives a young attorney a valuable perspective on criminal law.

Most prosecutors' offices are in or next to the courthouse, and you meet both experienced prosecutors and defense attorneys. Working in the prosecutor's office will give you a chance to meet the movers and shakers in law enforcement, including police chiefs and judges. It is a great networking opportunity. You learn how prosecutors, police, medical examiners – everyone helping to put together a case against a defendant – do their jobs. You gain insight into the people you will one day go up against as a criminal defense attorney, learning how they think and getting experience you could never get in law school.

Another great place to start is in the public defender's office. You will have constant work, landing in the middle of the action right away. Your services are sorely needed, you will be helping people, and you will be handling a variety of criminal cases.

Young lawyers pick up many valuable skills by starting out in the public defender's office, not the least of which is learning how to juggle many cases at one time. In addition, you will develop the confidence you need early in your career to present a case in court. You will also learn how to prepare witnesses for court hearings and how to deal with clients, especially those with difficult personalities.

Some young lawyers view working for a public defender's office as a calling and decide to make a career out of it. Many public defenders' offices across the country offer internships, and that is one of the best ways to see if you enjoy this type of work.

You can also start out as an associate at a midsize or large private law firm. Competition for these jobs is tough, and young associates in many of these private law firms do not get a chance to present a case in court for quite some time.

One of the first decisions you will make as a criminal defense lawyer is where you want to practice. You might find it beneficial to work in the same geographic area (city, county, and the like) for your entire career, making the most of the contacts and working relationships you cultivate in that region.

Networking is important in this field. Become active with your local and state bar associations, especially when you are first starting out. That can open many doors early in your career and get you known in the right legal circles. Even with all the social networking today, word-of-mouth advertising is still the best way to cultivate business. People trust a personal recommendation.

ASSOCIATIONS

■ **National Association of Criminal Defense Lawyers (NACDL)**
https://www.nacdl.org

■ **National Legal Aid & Defender Association (NLADA)**
http://www.nlada.org

■ **American Bar Association (ABA)**
http://www.americanbar.org/aba.html

■ **Association of Federal Defense Attorneys (AFDA)**
www.afda.org

■ National Lawyers Association (NLA)
http://www.nla.org

■ Association of Defense Trial Attorneys (ADTA)
https://adtalaw.com

■ National Bar Association
https://www.nationalbar.org

■ The National Trial Lawyers
www.thenationaltriallawyers.org

■ DUI Defense Lawyers Association (DUIDLA)
http://duidla.org

PERIODICALS

■ The Champion
Criminal Law Journal
The Oregon Criminal Defense Attorney Journal
The Trial Lawyer
Criminal Justice Magazine
The Journal of Criminal Law and Criminology
American Criminal Law Review
New Criminal Law Review
National Law Journal
The American Lawyer
Trial
The American Journal of Criminal Law

SCHOOLS

■ **University of Virginia School of Law**
www.law.virginia.edu/html
/academics/practical/criminaldefense.htm

■ **The University of Connecticut School of Law**
www.law.uconn.edu/academics/clinics-experiential
-learning/criminal-law-clinics

■ **Northwestern University Pritzker School of Law**
www.law.northwestern.edu/legalclinic/about

WEBSITES

■ **HG.org**
https://www.hg.org/aboutus.html

■ **American College of Trial Lawyers**
https://www.actl.com

■ **The American Law Institute**
https://www.ali.org

■ **Defense Research Institute (DRI)**
https://www.dri.org

■ **American Bar Association Criminal Justice Section**
www.americanbar.org/groups/criminal_justice.html

■ **Boston College Online Law School Locator**
http://www.bc.edu/offices/careers
/gradschool/law/research.html

■ Law Street
http://lawstreetmedia.com/schools
/law-school-specialty-ratings-2015

■ Association of American Law Schools (AALS)
http://www.aals.org

■ National Criminal Defense College (NCDC)
http://www.ncdc.net

■ Southern Poverty Law Center (SPLC)
http://www.splcenter.org

■ American Association for Justice
https://www.justice.org

CAREERS REPORTS
www.amazon.com/author/careers

CAREERS INTERNET DATABASE
www.careers-internet.org

Information
service@careers-internet.org